Praise for *A Natural History of Unnatural*

By unfurling the lush yet brittle-bone language of his art practice onto the page, Zachari Logan has crafted a record of *smaller worlds*, of elegiac *gardens of skin* and loss, of impermanence and beauty. *A Natural History of Unnatural Things* is infused with the same idiosyncratic attentiveness that characterises Logan's visual work; his is a vision that is simultaneously up-close and panoptic.

Sylvia Legris

At times intimate and diaristic, at others raw and abrasive, Logan's poems insistently blur the boundaries between reality and dreamscape, drawing the reader deeper into a richly evocative, perceptual realm. Line after line, each poem weaves a web of alternative relativities where human and non-human are enmeshed, inescapably caught in awesome interdependency. Recurring figures, circumstances, and conversational fragments outline an existentialist journey where materiality exudes desire. Logan's ability to tease the numinous out of the mundane is only one of the many gifts pressed between the pages of this book. As time and space collapse into a universe of visionary landscapes, one becomes aware that Logan's poetry belongs to the kind that forever changes the reader's perspective on the world. An experimental take on romantic post-humanism, *A Natural History of Unnatural Things* has its roots firmly planted in the dirt as its tendrils soar towards the sky, where waxy blooms and nectarine delights remind us that every minute in life is well worth savoring.

Giovanni Aloi
author of *Lucian Freud Herbarium* (2019, Prestel) and *Speculative Taxidermy: Natural History, Animal Surfaces, and Art in the Anthropocene* (2017: Columbia University Press)

Poetry and visual art have an intimate relationship, and the brilliant artist Zachari Logan demonstrates just how magnificent the exchange of imagery can be in his stunning debut poetry collection, *A Natural History of Unnatural Things*. In Logan's hands, the imprint of a moth wing on a napkin, or a loose tooth, or a cast-off cat claw in an ashtray can have heart-wrenching, macrocosmic ramifications. Combining the natural with the human-made, these poems become assemblages as complex as the horticultural collages of Mary Delany that Logan reveres. *A Natural History of Unnatural Things* reminds us that poetry comes from the kaleidoscopic imagination, yet it is Logan's life experiences that ground the wisdom of these always unpredictable, sumptuously precise, unflinchingly observed poems.

Molly Peacock
author of *The Paper Garden, Flower Diary* and *The Analyst: Poems*

In *A Natural History of Unnatural Things*, Zachari Logan draws on art, culture, travel and personal experience to portray his vision, using surreal and startling images that force leaps in the imagination. The poems range from finely honed lyrics to spare imagistic poems (in couplets) to prose-poem meditations rich with horror images often drawn from dreams or dreamlike memories. Here is a poet who comes with his first collection of poems that packs a lifetime experience from his reimagined birth to his meeting with his gay lover to somewhat droll eco-friendly conjectures about what he wants done with his body after his death, and all this considered in the larger context of our Homo sapiens evolutionary roots followed into a dystopic present.

gillian harding-russell
author of *Uninterrupted* and *In Another Air*

A NATURAL HISTORY
OF UNNATURAL THINGS

Copyright @ 2021 Zachari Logan

All rights reserved. No part of this publication may be reproduced, stored in a retrieval system or transmitted, in any form or by any means without the prior written permission of the publisher or by licensed agreement with Access: The Canadian Copyright Licensing Agency (contact accesscopyright.ca).

Editor: Adrienne Gruber
Cover art and illustrations: Zachari Logan
Book and cover design: Tania Wolk, Third Wolf Studio
Printed and bound in Canada at Friesens, Altona, MB

The publisher gratefully acknowledges the support of Creative Saskatchewan, the Canada Council for the Arts and SK Arts.

Library and Archives Canada Cataloguing in Publication

Title: A natural history of unnatural things / Zachari Logan.
Names: Logan, Zachari, 1980- author.
Description: Poems.
Identifiers: Canadiana 20210277599 | ISBN 9781989274538 (hardcover)
| ISBN 9781989274545 (softcover)
Classification: LCC PS8623.O369 N37 2021 | DDC C811/.6—dc23

radiant press

Box 33128 Cathedral PO
Regina, SK S4T 7X2
info@radiantpress.ca
www.radiantpress.ca

for Ned.

(also for Lil and Ash)

A NATURAL HISTORY
OF UNNATURAL THINGS

ZACHARI LOGAN

radiant press

I

2	This is Where It Ends
3	Virgo Moon
4	The Comet
5	Bouquet
6	Boxes
7	Danae to Perseus
9	Horror Poem: Streetscape
10	Ontological Stance
11	The Disappearing Sky
13	Liquid Clock
14	Grasslands
15	Flatline
16	The Loneliest Animal
17	Tattoo
18	Flowering
19	The Wake of Reason
20	Resurrection on Short Mountain
21	Late Afternoon
22	Empty Vase
23	The Grave of Oscar Wilde
24	The City Named for a Berry
24	I. Winter
26	II. Fall
27	III. Summer
28	IV. Spring

II

30	Invasive Species
31	Horror Poem: Web
32	Shimmer
33	Telemarketers
34	The Other Side
36	Datura
38	Ssssst!
40	Crown

41	Faerie Tale
42	Your Thoughts of a Harp
43	Luna
44	The Weight of the World is as Light as a Leaf
45	God-font
46	1984
47	Silhouettes
48	Muscle Flowers
49	Tooth
51	Softer Yellow
52	The Two Most Beautiful Buildings

III

56	No Small Crime
58	Sleepy City
59	Debussy and The Sea
60	Migraine
62	Posture
63	Night Vision
64	Chasms
65	Doubt carves a thistle
66	Giusti Gardens, Verona
67	Voice
69	Sad Torso
70	The Cloud Spitter
71	Horror Poems: Orphanage
72	Somewhere
74	Atrophy
75	Mary Delany's Hands
76	Four Years Before It Was Legal
77	The Last Bus
78	Things to Remember When I Die
81	Paper, Petals, Leaves and Skin: A Chance Encounter With the Affectionate Eye of Mary Delany

I

My bones; steel rods beneath the sea,
burning rigid sapphire into life.

This is Where It Ends

Garden of slow burning
ancient bodies.

Carpet of rides
without air.

Long skirt, cutting the ankle
at the right length.

Slow cinematic apocalypse,
eco-friendly, in full swing.

Peacock feather print
cascading downward
to the ground —

and through the lung,

A mouth
always leading to a belly.

You can't step
outside yourself

to become yourself.

Virgo Moon

September fills boxes.
A wounded soldier
saturates a dresser drawer.
A photograph's edges
smell of vinegar.

Clever moon—
In my mother's body
you cradled me with a crescent,
found a way for my birth
to be one month late.

I remember my grandmother's bony hands
withered with the dread of forgetting.
Cover your feet, she'd say, tucking me in
at night, *or the devil will pinch them
while you sleep.*

Wide awake, with toes discreetly
out of sight, I'd stare out the window
at the trees, abandoning the cool green
for a warmer coat,
leaves yellowing like his skin
to greet the Virgo moon.

The Comet

Infinity; ocular ribbon.
No voice-over
placebo.

Bouquet

MRI measures whirling decay.
Our most intimate bits
forge a grey mass of values.
A dancing greyscale of diagonal telling,
cloning our experiences for the magnificence
of an indefinite timeline.

So often stuck in the moment
when a burn feels like a rush
of cold water.

The mind telling the body,
it's not as bad as it actually is.

A bouquet of cut limbs,
planted across my back.
Green fringe of thumbs
incapable of amputation.

There are no spaces
between blood and healing.

Boxes

I once received a wheel-mechanized Cookie Monster. The kinetic toy had a cookie-filled hand that lifted to the oversized mouth of the cartoon figure as an attached string pulled the toy along. I gleefully carried the box around for a week, ignoring the petrol-blue effigy it housed.

I must have seen a commercial for the toy, but I can't recall it. I imagine a child actor pulling it through the outskirts of astroturf, ants poking through underneath. Incomprehension borne of bright plastic toys, harnessed by the suburban skin of childhood.

Mopic glowing advertisements shed by sunlight through a threaded ozone. So many empty boxes off-gassing cardboard monsters under the skirts of my bed.

I was seven when I awoke to the unfurling of grass I'd been trampling.

All those smaller worlds at my feet.

Danae to Perseus

My liver-hearth boils down toxins
for a radiant gilded Zeus.

Gold coins protrude from my stomach
greasy, pliant discs caress tensed muscles,
like snakelets wriggle from a pregnant serpent.

Set adrift on something liquid,
a vast landscape of prophesy
and disappointment.

Small wooden boxes
that are not waterproof.
Savings for things; Checkings for things.
Arranging for things.

The assets: a blue depth.
This new colour leaves the world
underneath; always pithy.

Crash of a thousand
stock exchanges
reverberate in my bronze room,
and the *Wall Street Journal* declaims:
"Money Isn't Real:
It's Your Soul that's Sold."

I read this
and warn you,
Go my child,
evade the gaze of the bull.
You are invisible—
but you do exist inside
the herald's shoe.

Be a shadow
and bring me back
that melted down skull.

Horror Poem: Streetscape

Tree roots moan, audible
beneath porous road tar.
Single shriek conjured from
a Bosch painting of damnation
and chimney-stack sex.
Something cognizant scurries away
to troglodyte festivities,
hosted under asphalt sheets,
by inanimate objects
and body parts.

Ontological Stance

Metallic centipede cascades
gracefully. A warning
of pain to come.

My loved ones wish me
to remember my father in
bedside flurries,
an ontological stance.

I am a result of joy,
lust and evolution.
I can't place things.

They're stored inside bones
that ache, and even now
crackle in
and out of joint.

The Disappearing Sky

She points out the window
and says, *there's a shape like dried wildflowers
in the sky...*

At first I think she means
a cloud.

I look up and see only a deep blue pool,
then, just to the right of my periphery,

liquid mercury;
a twirling nebulous pendant.

Are they tulips? I ask, narrowing my eyes.

No, she says, *dried tulips look like
arthritic hands, petals bending every which way
as they crisp up.*

An eclipse of shape shifting
rose hip, or dandelion. We cannot tell
exactly what it is. The sun's
embers deep in our optic nerve.

We did see something, though.
I don't think anyone else did.

Overlapping tree limbs
code meaning. Flung shadows
scripting the air above us.

*The disappearing sky
has emerged in time lapse* she says
*over centuries,
one thousand lifetimes.*

*Humans floating around
the cinema, specs of dust moving in
and out of projected light.*

*Each of us a mind
like a can of condensed milk,
one dent and the milk sours.*

Liquid Clock

An ocean floor
leviathan,
distills a deep
recess of everywhere
you've been.

Jellyfish plasma
scroll graffiti forgeries
across artery walls.

Grasslands

Chest hair furls the top
of a white t-shirt.
Bunches of unkempt grass
spew over a bleached fence.

Summer tasting air
conducts a dance
on a hairy patch
of earth.

Sun leaps
scribbling
linear shadows.

Flatline

Bellini's beet-faced putti
over-shoulder,
remind me that perceiving colour
is no passive activity.

Reddish-peach; bruised
apricot; anemic yellow
seeps in.

Goethe gazing
into the troposphere
witnessing light
and dark dance
the embrace
of self-extinction.

A fiery-orange flatline,
just before the gloaming.

The Loneliest Animal

Walks the earth
knowing more
and more.

An unnatural history
of natural things.
The question *why*,
a constant companion.

Scullion
of geography and sky.

So genetically similar
to rodent, pig
and maze,
only experimentation
and consumption
can differentiate.

Conceptual beast;
brainy; singing vulnerable
offspring to sleep.

Evolving
a twin appendage —
melancholy and hunger.

Shedding skin
for hide,
cotton, linen, silk
and plastic.

Tumble dry on low
in a fugitive garden.

Tattoo

I once had someone
puncture words in my arm.

The font lay vertical,
a large vein
inducing life below,
blurring crisp lines
that scabbed over.

Layered by convention,
the ink sat
beneath my skin,
mute,

until spoken,
not by a voice,

but by the brushing
of your beard
on my arm.

Flowering

I lay on the sweating grass,
imagine my testicles
as downy green
poppy pods.
Tiny apertures
uncloaking
crimson-furrowed
petals.

Fondling discreetly
over my shorts,
I clutch a coated wad
of wormy varicoceles.
Achy elastic roots,
re-formed
by the certainty
of gravity and a lack
of sun.

The Wake of Reason
for Goya

Two hundred and seventy-year-old seer
laughs at the awkward footing
of a modern man attempting
a medieval dance.

A desert of poppy-eyed
outcomes. Blazing
and opiated.

Statehood becomes fertilizer
for the prolapsing glare
of a strongman.

Bats flee an etching,
only to be greeted
by the blinding sun,

Single dog
peers fatefully
over a hill
at one hundred seconds
to midnight.

Resurrection on Short Mountain

Gary leaves a bat carcass on the floor for us. An ironic gift, like roses at a funeral, his bat is useless to us—but comforting. He could live abundantly outside in the Tennessee mountains, but he has accepted us. A domesticated family.

I think about drawing its miniature limbs and teeth. Three days of humidity and heat transform the tiny creature to a bloated mass. The bat's head bobs up, then to the side. As if break-dancing, one leg jets up in the air and begins to turn. Two enormous beetles emerge, like ghosts from the book of Ecclesiastes, one from its mouth, the other from its ass.

After eating a large portion of its innards, they've made a bed of its body and laid eggs within it. Rotten and animated by the living, with fluorescent orange striped backs and heads crowned with gold tinted helmets.

A few weeks later, like the end of a morning church service, the larvae open the doors of the collapsing body and emerge.

Late Afternoon

Summer perspires
on dusk coloured burdock,
and the back alley dusting
of herbicide indemnities.

While Republicans flirt
with fascist boots, on
fashionable belted police.

Empty Vase

Stem-bruised water
a condo of upturned
bugs.

Cellophane wings on
tiny black dots.

The Grave of Oscar Wilde

In Paris there is a claret moss of lipstick
climbing the grave of Oscar Wilde.

Thousands of mouths inflame the same stone,
each a solitary kiss of alien lamentation.

His epitaph in granite engraved
from the scars of internment.

City of lights, a closet of stars,
first glanced from the depths of a gutter.

The City Named for a Berry

I. Winter

Green jerseys, homophobes, racists, ugly politicians and a hungry mayor. Beautiful streets. A speedy river dividing east and west– joined by crumbling bridges. This city is a petulant child.

Everyone sleeping in their cars. Living in their cars. A whole city lived in cars. Insects crossing one another on the road, hard endoskeletons, fleshy bits cozy inside. Exposure turns bitter cold into smoulder, skin peeling flake-by-flake.

Single-dwelling cars dilute the origin of slick black crude, billowing pre-historic exhaust. Blue blanket of anti-freeze bleeds onto concrete, paved for a future scrawled in reflective paint. There are more parking stalls than beds. Isolation is shouldered by street lamps and recycling containers; paper, glass, cardboard, plastic, tin, fabric, computer parts, solitude.

This city cradles all the complaining farmers who used to fence it. Suburbia functioning better now than it did when I grew up inside its shoe. Breadbasket of Wal-Mart box-stores, stale coffee, outlet mall exhaustion, and public washroom sex.

The repetition of city transit driven by a union of wintery trolls. Brazen to bridges and pavement. The silvery reflection of rain, softening the compact of solid snow layers, then hardening again under the shaman boots of the city. Taking the trail along the river back to their realtors, always purchasing more places to live, to evolve, to flip. Never content with the companionship of plaster walls, fruit flies and silverfish.

I live behind Cathedral row. This is the wildest part of the city. Crayfish, frozen just underneath the banks of the river. Jackrabbits, magpies, and the odd nomadic coyote all squat here, unaffected by the perennial futility of a city that thinks itself eternal.

Often mistaken for loss, there is no transition here. Simply change; and a string of Indigenous men left outside the city, barefoot, frozen.

II. Fall

Bus rides weave accidents out of bones and tree-trunks, stealing hours, leaving me idle to think of you. The milk-thistle on my arm forcing you up through the gravel with its root, while the rest of this city's people overhead, floating upside-down. An aquarium full of dead fish, the Bessborough, our castle in the bedrock.

Sifting through nine months, minus a day. The headline about a baby a young girl left in the trash. A coital remnant; and now likely below, petrified in potash. Leaves are the real missing persons in this town, each one on the back of a milk carton.

After enough time, Eden becomes a tomb. Sleeping beetles lose their homes to the fingernails of an anxious child. Scratch out a tunnel in the dirt, hard as bone in November. The concrete walls of basement suites absorb memories; underneath, mining possibility in the places where we come up.

III. Summer

Drunk on co-dependence and nocturnal valium, beauty hemorrhages in the warmth we never get used to. Lost intuition about what is coming or what has just left. Collective amnesias shit on every door-step. The heat makes this city forget itself in the performance of living.

Exhausted in a theatre of manmade lakes, paved riverfronts and water wasted by the tonne, offered up to regimes of sprinkler totalitarianism. Mistaking insects illuminated by fluorescent bulbs for fireflies disappearing into the frolic of black.

I remember sex for the first time with another boy on a gravel bed, and then the silence that contained it. Dried semen and tiny pebbles stuck to my leg, abetting the persistence of awkward memories. His response, shame, the incapability to feel shame, my own.

Everyone wants to be here during the time I'd like most to leave.

IV. Spring

Thaw slips into the long run of highway tragedies; porcupine, raccoon, deer, moose. The odd human. Carcasses soften our memory to the arcane stench of life.

Objectivity rests on something undefined, skipping naively towards nothing. The air gets grittier, earthier, emergent. Confidence sprouts, but remains close to the ground, appealing the sun without exposing its neck.

The wealthy snowbirds are back. All the winged creatures, along with the aggressive Canadian geese honking awkwardly a song of shadows as they pass overhead.

II

You are every character in your dream.
Your dreams never reveal the plot.

Invasive Species

Sidewalks billow generations
of dandelions out of concrete mouths,
made smaller by the gravity of glass
and steel beaming, the
grey sky turned violet.

Breathy and coffee stained,
my smile clothed in a frown.
Posture like Saint George, creeping
into the dragon's cave. A chest
full of hot air and soot, spilling out
into the South Saskatchewan.

The expanse of prairie grasslands
in sways and orchestras
of Horned Red-Dock, Yellow Star Thistle
and Wind Witch, revealing so many pages
of land. Songs sung long before partitioning,
theft and the piling of bones.

Tiny pebbles and glass imbedded
on my knee, braille for ever-present
timelines. My skin reveals veins that resemble
rivers on a map. I trace them, trying to locate
a less invasive vascularity.

Horror Poem: Web

Multi-eyed
panoptic glow.
Arachnid
bowel uncoils fear of
headless progress.

Shimmer

I dreamt a parallel me was

painting a self-portrait. The likeness

was based on a shadow cast by us both moving

quickly across a shimmer. The liquid unfolded us in the

slippage of gravity. I picked up the brush and added something

obscure.

> (I can't recall what it was. I often forget these
> sorts of details.)

Telemarketers

His son and three daughters disliked visiting him since their mother died a year ago. It had been three months, in fact, since any of them ventured the 15 miles out of town to sit in silence and endure the uncomfortable exchange of words.

He listened to the solicitations of 'drones on phones', as he was fond of calling them. He appreciated their voices —their breathing audible, from opposite ends of the earth, India, Pakistan, the Philippines.

He argued incessantly about anything, other than the reason they'd called. Their accents, the weather, his failing bowels. His favourite times of the day were 9am, 1pm and 7pm, when they most frequently rang.

Lately, there had been a slough of electronic calls.

The Other Side

The morning your breath left you,
the nurse says, *it's time*.
Your toes hard as granite.
Garden of skin
blooming bright yellow.
Pre-mature autumn,
followed by a Virgo sky.

I hadn't even thought of a way
to say goodbye.

Six in the morning sinking six feet
into ordinary sheets. The nurse crying
at the door to your hospital room—
reminds me of the day
our family cat was killed.
Her little head cocked back,
skull broken,
an eyeball dangling like
a milky red marble.

I took her tiny body in my hands,
turning her over to find the other side
unharmed. Her grey tabby fur cradled
my unflinching dread.
You told me to put her in the bin out back,
but I wrapped her in my plaid winter scarf
and buried her behind the lilacs.

I pull back the sheet, reveal
your dying transformation.

I can't turn you over
to find the other side unharmed.
I lay across your belly,
a stiff flaxen mound of flesh.

Datura

With a butter knife, I dug your bed.

I bled on the dry dirt.

You with those bluish leaves, and I
with the reticent hopes of a new gardener.

I will miss your spectre.
A small weed when I planted you.

The night of your first bloom
I waited for you to unfold
from a sharp lavender coil
into a white trumpet.
Your casing shed like
a loose pair of green trousers.

I knew then, you had planted me.

In the nocturne, adjusted eyes
see your purpose. Swollen orbs; blooming remnant,
a prickle of utility,
split open to the spill
of reoccurrence.

We are precarious together.
There's a simplicity in our epoch,
quickening of skins; green, juicy,
bluing and pinkish.

To ingest even a small amount
of your blossom, seed, or stock,
brings death, or possibly
a two-week delirium.

Some attempt to harvest your meaning-
tearing at your robust limbs.

It is likely the cold that makes them heartless,
impatient. I won't mourn their trouble.

But Datura, I will find your bloom
in the brassy wakefulness
of winter.

Outside my window, twelve heads
at the height of your dominion,
myriad dragon.

Ssssst!

Film noir florals on Dekalb.
Drunk rain steams from
cluttered rooftops.

The sway of jutting iron follows
seven million steps along the Hudson.

The song the subway cars make
are years of shuffling shoes
within a single *ssssst!*

Shoreline spits you
back on land, belly swollen.
Metallic loop undertow.
Stop along the way
for distractions' sake to read
the latest maintenance notification
taped to a vintage sway,
on a dull piece of paper.

Midnight lulls cockroach plots.
West 4th Street lighting
pardons our lack of sleep
on Malcolm X Boulevard.

You lay there as a greenish glow
paints a diamond on your contour,
illuminating a cluster of shoulder hair.
Blades of grass invoked by electricity
and circumstance.

Peer through useless curtains
to empty-handed, wordy streets.
Waking dreams left
by the absence of sleep;
brick-lined mornings,
the womb noise
of burnished overground snakes.
New York City scatters
her children onto salty pavement.

Crown

Put your ear
to the ground
to hear a rock split.

Walk on land,
bejewelled by pot-hole
capillaries
and a dam.

Slip into
the leftover territory,
like a thrift store bargain
and watch the sun set
on your shadow.

Inspired by the writing of Jean Teillet, in particular:
The Northwest Is Our Mother: The Story of Louis Riel's People, The Metis Nation.

Faerie Tale

A peanut butter knife through
warm margarine,
we split the road in half.

Sitting on the side of the highway,
watching you piss down a coulee
into the mouth of good intention—

cutting lizard tails
to watch them grow back.

Your Thoughts of a Harp

Imagine where blood goes
once it's replaced with embalming fluid.
Into a drain.

So that the people attending your funeral
can stand to look at an un-animated veracity.

The dead present for the living what they really are.

Funerals are not for the body dressed in old clothing—
if they were, disintegration would be respected.
Futures denied.

I wish I'd left my dad in the hospital bed;
yellow mass of flesh, neck-muscles pooling
into shoulders, sweat evaporating into sockets,
stones in place of what moments before
were eyes. Pain and life disappearing.

It was the moment I felt most animal in my whole life.
And this is what we are.

Death brings us down off our clouds.
Says, this is *your* future.

Fuck you and your thoughts of a harp.

Luna

A moth wing's thread
glows the moon. Dusted
minute flickers of pattern.
Owl eyes mirror back
to owl, with lunar eggs
laid.

The Weight of the World is as Light as a Leaf

Another discarded cat claw
on the sill,

to be placed
in the antique candy bowl.

Stale-air, a witch's brew
of whiskers,
claws,
fortune cookie scrolls,
dried orchid blooms,
daffodils

and a leaf.

Thanatos grips
the piling of twigs,
onto leaves,
grass,
stones;

bedskirts for many frozen
months.

A long ago thought
you birthed,
manifests as a drop
in temperature.
A brisk wind

causes a condensation,
cataract on the window
panes; light and movement
divined
through the gaze
of an augur.

God-font

Fingertip-stained
vignette edges
acrid-free pages.

The colour of marrow,
brain matter
in god-font.

1984

Ramona flops on her bed,
laughing at our brother Gavin.

My arm extends slightly
under hers—but comfortably
as we bounce.

Daniel by Elton John
is playing.

A purple plastic heart
hangs from the bedroom ceiling

slowly twirling above us.

Silhouettes

He walks his neighbourhood during the day while most people are at work. A gentrified section of the city going through yet another process of forgetting.

His apartment is across the street from a small, rarely inhabited park that was once an industrial glass-works factory. The name of the park is the namesake of the old factory; a reference neither he nor his neighbours would know.

This quarter used to be filled with geometric red-brick factories, now, geometric red-brick condominiums, and a spattering of commercial carrion spaces not yet divided among the city-planning crows. Cavernous places, popular among young professionals. Spaces in which to be alone.

The odd night he walks the park as well. Through the windows of his neighbours' homes, he sees their silhouettes as they sit immobile, huddled in front of flat screens, losing their eyesight to an ancient flicker of light.

Muscle Flowers

1

Stems, bending bipedal,
sculpted to puff out the chest,
displaying a riff at the top of the spine.

Erect, heterosexual shoulders,
scented by noxious chemicals.

> (Are you worried
> your smell might be
> arousing to other muscle flowers?)

2

We are all admired
by the queerness
of the light spectrum.

You don't catch
'The Gay';
you either are,
or you are not.

Tooth

I have a tooth that
fools me.

It creeps out in front of the others.
It is loose.

At night, while I sleep it ventures,
a forest of portents and unnamed borders.
It collects things.

Cavities-
doorstops for my mouth.

A reoccurring dream:
I've fallen from high up
shattering every tooth but it.
When I wake,

dry mouth.
It is the only point on my head
unfixed.

With my index and thumb
I attempt to push it
flush with its neighbours.

Alien roots deeper than the rest.
White trees, thickets of
porcelain poplar,
aim up and down.

I gape as it creeps out in front of the others.
I have a tooth that fools me.

It wants me to say words
I'd rather eat.

Softer Yellow

Today is decorated
in another year's wallpaper.

Working from home
with roll over eyes
and bed-sheet surveillance.
2-ply freshener, cat-litter toes
and drainage. Watching wifi stories
filter hi-def ideologies.

No commercials.
You are the ad.

War of the rosettes, in soft yellow
and platelet burgundy, repurposed
from the magazine pile.

Appliances without warrantee
made of shiny plastic,
in softer yellow
reflecting chrome misogyny
and vacuum bag phobias.

The Two Most Beautiful Buildings
for Lorca

For an entire month I walked clear past
the two most beautiful buildings in the world.
Cobblestone Medusas and vineyards of glass beads.
Nacht Macht drenched in pigeon shuffles,
original paintings, thought to be prints.

Ghost of Klimt haunts every souvenir shop.
Plated gold envy and cheap bone china gazing
and gazing. Hungarian waiters jousting goulash
and schnapps, in search of periphery chairs.
Sit in a room of overflowing ashtrays.

A museum of fakes, shelter the real ones
entombed below. Durer and Schongauer and Maximilian I
fortifying dampness, bloodied and whispering
paper-cut witches. Stephensdom emerges limestone
mansion, from a heap of 11th century serfs,
concave master coils up and down.

On chalky vertebrae, I stood towering.
Babel of black bone fragments.
Terrains gilded with the bustle of Wagner's ceramic
poppies, violets. Ormolu and roses bursting through, yet
obscured by pink and black marble.

Duplication filigree topple brick guts,
humming the gorge of squeeze-box refrains.
The absurd drama of Catholic saints.
Vienna, open mouthed. Catching breath,
closes a smile full of sooty buildings.

Surfacing a calm street of endless
passageways. Café combustion threatens
the green glow of nicotine. A cluster
of Breughel's flat-footed peasants,
one North American foot
in front of the other.

III

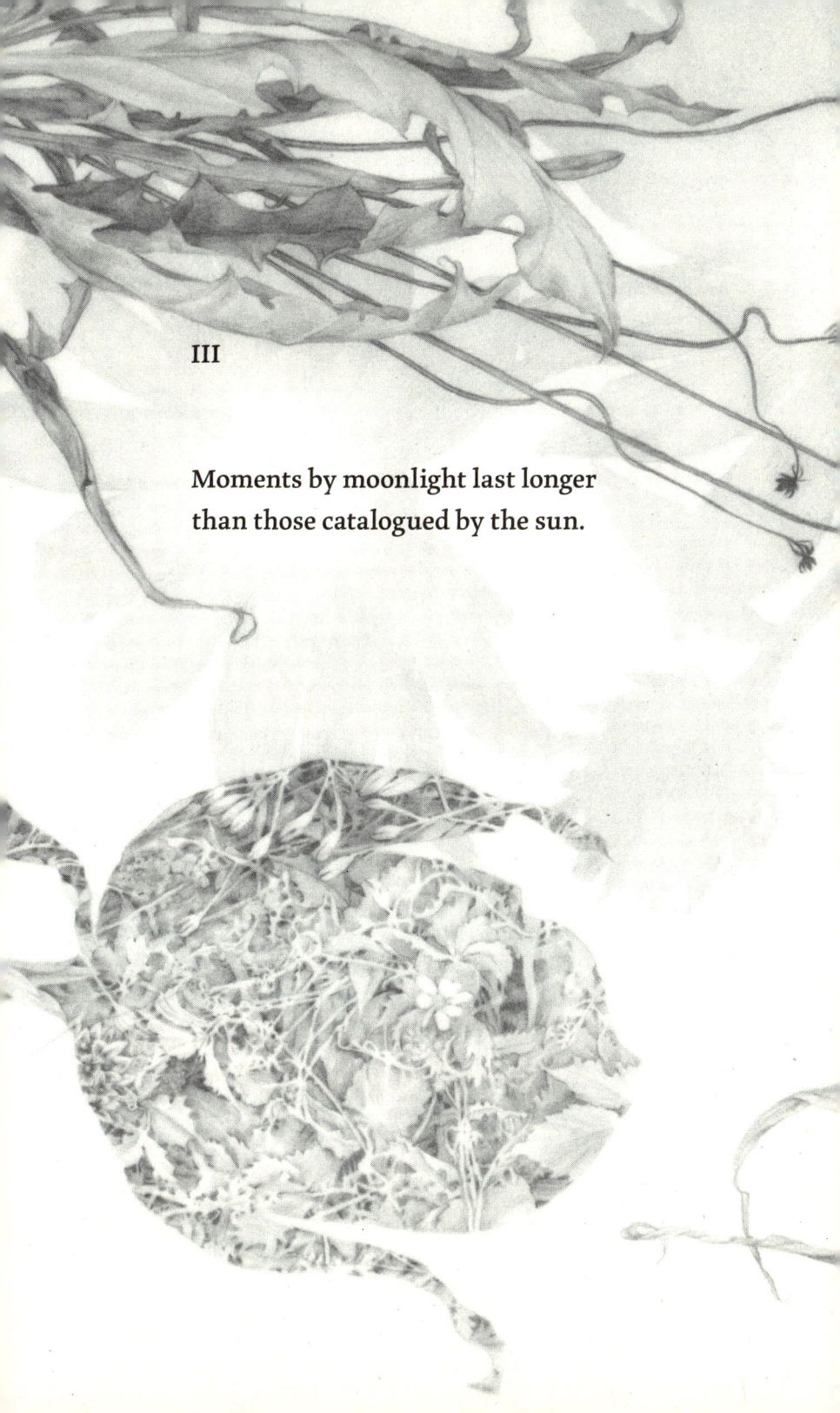

Moments by moonlight last longer
than those catalogued by the sun.

No Small Crime

A white moth lands in the middle of my palm, filling the centre of it, dancing in a slight shift, one left-sided limb flits back and forth on either side of my lifeline. Antennae above her cloth wings wave like grass.

She must feel the warmth of me, like the sun on a dark coloured stone. I examine her, note the slight movements for the intake of breath; the tiniest of implosions. Moths don't have lungs, I learn later in a biology class, but tube-like openings called spicules.

She is enormous; beautiful, a fabulous queen moth Liberace. There must be something sweet on my hand because she won't fly away—not even when I try to toss her gently into the sky like a maple seed. I take her inside with me.

She becomes very still, while my hand rests inside my desk, rolling back and forth on pencil crayons through a lesson of math, then history, then afternoon recess. Surely she will feel the wind's fingers under her furriness and this will hurry her along, but no, just a slight shimmer in her silvery abdomen.

Perfectly centred in my palm like a queer stigmata, she grants me the wonder of the sky. I try once more to lift her, this time gingerly, with my pinky-finger, but she extends her legs up with the nudge of my fingernail. Her body says *no, not yet*.

Someone notices me staring at my hand. Before long,
a group of kids wants a turn holding her. As a circle of eyes
grew exponentially, I try to explain she does not belong to
me. A finger-tap on my shoulder, an arm from the tent of
bodies reaches across, slapping my palm.

Before I can register the fate of my beautiful visitor, there is
a cold wetness on my hand and face, her bitter-tasting guts
on my tongue. I'm shoved to the ground; a mixture of dirt,
tears, and blood coalescing her pearly innards in my mouth.
I gulp a breath of air, swallow bits of this violence, and spit
outwards into the sky.

Her iridescent eggs, and one perfectly dusted wing slips off
the edge of my hand's web. A microcosmic cruelty,
but no small crime. A stream of seraphic spit in the centre
of my palm dries like raw egg in the wind.

I pick her wing off the ground, keep it pressed tightly
between my index and thumb. I don't put it down for the
rest of the day, until dinner. I slide it under my plate for
safekeeping. The cool ceramic warms with the heat of my
meal. Condensation forms on the underside, disintegrating
the white wing. The tablecloth reveals a faint chalk outline.

Sleepy City

Buildings,
the city's children—

ghostly monuments survived by
memories alone.

Vestiges wilting
in and out of avenues
built on stillness.

Faster than people live

and die
in a single home.

Debussy and The Sea
Lido Beach, Venice, Italy. July 2019

I can hear the ocean
in the shell of you,
polishing
translucent waves
of slippery brass.

Plucked for a dangle,
a shimmer of earlobe hopes,
indulge a dressy whisper.

Music; pure math pearls form,
a sphere of watery sadness.

Migraine

Light's perpetual
                stirring.

Metallic smoke ring
ache.

Mercurized threads
                    spool
layers of glossy shard.

Zigzag through   peripheries.

Blue-grey slate fragment,

then a sanguine red,
purple slides limpid into mustard
dried paint,
        mixed on a long-ago palette,
store-bought white

Kaleidoscopic thumb
into my eyeball.

Swirling god-wreath
of Hildegard von Bingen
swims closer, then past—
throttles me
        on a single minute spot.

Porcelain fissures
                zero-zero three
opens like the red sea,

dive head-first

into the shallow end.

Posture

My father's backbone coils in a box
like trinkets arch around the neck.

Night Vision

Insect flickers dim
a lit corridor. Joan of Arc
spoke to herself under
a similar moon.

Chasms

The attic of his mind
a lock-box chest of boney
misplaced happenings.
Mounds of dusty Victorian toys,
awkward composite of kinetic
mechanical irregularities—
clumpy segments
of taxidermy fur.

Remembering was walking over
a creaky wooden bridge
held together by bristly threadbare ropes.

A children's picture book
with half the pages missing.

He catches glimpses of colour
or design, where the ripped paper
joined the exposed spine
of the book.

Doubt carves a thistle

out of the crawlspace
in your head.

Giusti Gardens, Verona

Mislaid in plain sight
on a quotidian street,
as hidden worlds
often are.

The stooped portico
exists for a single chandelier pendant.

Warm light melts frost
formed in a sagittal
across alpine limbs.

The adjoining
conifers line a central walkway,
leading to a steep climb.

Labyrinthian cloister
dances a maze of shrubs
ten generations long,
propelling us into
the gargoyle's mouth.

Sun beams warmth
on moss and ferns. We reach
the top of the world.

Through Titian's atmospheric eye,
a pastoral concert under the loggia
of a Verona sky.

Voice

His body language caused a stir in the room, a dumb parity of furled brows. What is he thinking? He's mid-sentence into explaining when the first deafening shot was fired.

This sudden jolt pierces the thick predictability of the room. As it passes through, a strange wetness tickles his forehead making its way down his face through a passage between his eyes.

A warm sting snakes its way down the back of his cranium, mirroring the trickle of wet dividing his face into two parallels; an infinite space. A sharp realness he'd experienced once before, but could not recall when. This odd continuity, felt in reality for only a millisecond, split his consciousness into two equal halves.

He feels the stage his feet are planted on suddenly uproot and spit him into the air. This involuntary thrust is accompanied by a misty hue of redness in his vision, and a loud barrage of incoherent sounds.

Pain submerged his body, flooding the most remote areas. An invisible pendulum passes through him into the floor he sprawls, then back out to the air of the open stage. With each migration, pain plunges him further into a grey obliterating fog.

Not aware the stretching of time, he somehow fades back into the misty-red hover. A familiar voice edges its way through the forest of commotion. The voice is calming, as if it were being broadcast through the bottom of a tub, in which he is submerged.

Sad Torso

Sunday morning recalls
the porcelain face
of my God-on-a-stick.
Spectre tumbling in my belly.

I think he was
my first love.

A lost limb,
haunting a sad torso.

I've eaten him
thousands of times by now,
absorbing nothing
but contempt.

The Cloud Spitter

I watch the cats from the bathtub
use our size twelve shoes to strategize
trench warfare,
the TV blaring stupidity.

Sink low into my bathwater,
fleshy submarine, I imagine a eulogy
for the buoyant ones.

I don't have to put you
in the ground anymore,
I can just spread you
on the circumference
of things.

Bodies of water
with their untidy depths.
All the exotic places
they could guide you to.

I am the cloud spitter,
gravity a valued employee.

Where would you like to go?

Horror Poems: Orphanage

My candles in my pocket,
I can sleep without a noise.

Bonfire in the basement,
smoke collapsing lungs.

Balloons shriek
evaporation.

Birthdays come, cluttered
green and gold.

I escape. Slipping off gravity's
chin, I hit the ground.

Solid fracture.

Bones float inside my shoe.
I limp like a stricken bird.

Clickety-clack, clickety-clack
my foot touching ground.

Watch through the window
as you eat my cake.

Somewhere

Between the scar of a dog bite on my left shoulder blade and a lacerated meniscus repair mending underneath; Wascana Lake cottonwoods and the Frontenac on Lorne; Gaudi's spiny Basílica and the Roman-faced stone fountains; Lower Clapton Road and Stanley Spencer's *The Resurrection, Cookham*—

Between Union Station and Queen Street West; Big Valley gravel and the Lethbridge coulees; La Cieniga Blvd. and the Koreatown lights; the Parthenon covered in wiry stray cats to the open fish market of Athens; the recline of Dublin's marble Oscar Wilde and the dusted tomb-studio of Francis Bacon; Sotoportego passageway to the lion reliefs of the Venice Hospital entrance.

Between the marble walls of the Kunsthistorisches and Danube river; the sidewalk cracks on Spadina Ave and the wind cutting through 20th Street at Avenue C; the Sleeping Giant and a small crumbly greenhouse on Sherwood Drive; via Salida XX Settembre and the Roman Theatre of Verona; the foot of the hill at Edinburgh Castle and Jenny Geddes cuttie-stool in St. Giles Cathedral.

Between Osborne Village and the Red River currents; Peachtree Road and Miami Circle NE; constellation Virgo and late blooming September wildflowers; Bernini's *Four Rivers* and the San Luigi Chapel; Place Des Arts to the encapsulated fragments of Saint Andre's heart; the foot of the Torre Velasca to Caravaggio's *Basket of Fruit* in the Biblioteca Ambrosiana.

Between Missinippi and Latrace Road; the incessant honking of East Houston and the quiet of Washington Heights; Murfreesboro suburbs and the pear farm on Short Mountain; the elbowing pinch of the Marais and the highest tip of Botzaris Park.

Between Ned's nightly read from the couch and the tickling whiskers of our old girl, Asherah.

Atrophy

Articulating frustration as a baby,
I locked joints, tensing muscles
to spasm.
This was my first—
best response to being.

When atrophy sets in,
I'll be a good tree.

Mary Delany's Hands
British Museum: Paper Archives Room, Nov. 16th, 2016

Speckled skin over
methodical bones.
Constellations composed
by the saturated
brush of sun
on archival paper.

Hands that bring forth
botanic lovers,
so quietly, so elegantly—

Petals yet unfurling
in my dewy sight.

I hold my breath
to the placement of perennial
lavender strips,
enveloped
into a tiny black pool.

Parchment irises
in-bloom,
tucked back into
midnight boxes.

Four Years Before It Was Legal

I asked you to be a prop
for my drag performance
of *Raspberry Swirl*.

I fed you
an apple.

The following week
we met for coffee
at the Broadway Roastery.
We talked about music.
I learned you had
Tori Amos and Joni Mitchell
in your CD binder.

The smell
of your coarse earthy
stubble. My lip's
stingy-swell.
The slightest
fricative,
almost unheard
even by me.

Three months
later, 4 AM, you

propose
we let our hair
grey together.

The Last Bus
for STC

Bladed between the Drumheller Hoodoos
and the yearly passion plays there.
A bottle of something soapy,
drank as if holy wine.

Engine idles, divining a sunlit corridor.
Below the cab-thrones of truckers
Immobile beside you,
However, well above the sedans.

You depend on these stilts
To see above their heads,
Scalps thinning to soft threads.

The last bus loads to follow
This windy script of road.

A panoptic tale.
Crow, owl, and magpie.
Sentinels of flattening land
and swelling skies.

Things to Remember When I Die

Put me back in the ground
Where I came up.
The garden of skin.

Bury me in the backyard
With the cats.
Keep me from
The masochistic whispers
Of graveyard sainthood.

Out of sight of watchful cobblestone glances.
Grace I want nothing to do with.

Every now and then
spill some coffee
into the earth for me.
An offering to an atheist.

The green blanket
six feet above, a receptor
for every salutation,
folding like dampened paper.
Years of forgetfulness.
Fathoms of poetic decay.

No miracles-
I plan to stay where I am,
a Lazarus for the twenty-first century.

Until one day someone
buries this poem
in the ground

and like a nymph
of the groundwater I
pull it to life underneath.

Paper, Petals, Leaves and Skin: A Chance Encounter With the Affectionate Eye of Mary Delany

In museums I find my humanity. The artworks I become enamoured with offer simple clues about their creators, and although are from vastly different times and places, their voice give me insight about the world in which I live. Studying collections, where space, time and place are contextually vital to the artworks themselves, often finds me in a dialogue with ghosts, and I suppose bits of myself. Growing-up on the Canadian prairies, I had less access to art I could readily see reproduced in books and had to imagine the actual physical presence an artwork might elicit. It was in this disposition to imagine or rather desire, that art books became hugely influential to me. I think about this quite a bit now in our present state of isolation because of COVID-19.

My exposure to actual collections in scale and quantity came later, but I quickly understood early in my practice that my role as a maker was contingent on my role as a viewer. The catalyst for information and transfer of ideas in my process is of my body and art history. To say that another way; the expressions of queerness I create as a consequence of thinking about embodiment, tie personal experience visually with art historical reference. Investigating artworks in terms of composition, line, colour, and stylistic technique did not slow or end for me after university, it became a more voracious extension of my research. Exposure to collections has meant continual engagement with artists and artworks from different periods, for different reasons.

Encounter
My first encounter with Mary Delany came by chance. I was in London for my first exhibition in the UK, and while there, I visited the famed British Museum. I recall wandering rather aimlessly through corridors of ancient artifacts: utensils for cooking/cleaning, body-parts, jewelry, weaponry, children's toys, a plaster-of-Paris death-mask of Napoleon Bonaparte; and then somewhere, placed seemingly by omission amongst the grandiose and grotesque, quietly hung two small botanicals. This wasn't a small room, nor is the British Museum a small collection, but, at the risk of sounding cliche, the world simply dissolved around me as I gazed at the small floral paper-works for over an hour. Mesmerized by their exactitude, scale and honesty I revisited them twice that day. I couldn't get them out of my mind.

I did however, want to know more about their creator. So I made my way to the gift shop in search of a title, and found two. Ruth Hayden's informative *Mrs Delany: Her Life In Flowers*, (Hayden herself a descendant of Delany's sister Anne); and Molly Peacock's *The Paper Garden*, a brilliant portrait of Delany, layered with autobiographical parallels of the poet herself. Mary Delany, born May 14th 1700, lived a fascinating life I would soon find out through these two texts, both wonderful primers for my budding infatuation with her.

I would meet Molly Peacock three years later in Toronto at the reception for *Bliss: Gardens, Real And Imagined*, an exhibition at the Textile Museum of Canada that included my drawing *Pool No. 2, after Mary Delany*. As a member of the museum she'd received an invite with a reproduction of the drawing. The title featuring Delany made Peacock curious, so she made a point of inquiring. By this time I'd dog-eared my copy of *The Paper Garden* to death, and so when Peacock introduced herself, I was somewhat in disbelief. She even attended my concurrent Toronto exhibition *Forgotten Selves* at Paul Petro Contemporary, and put me in contact with a lateral descendant of Delany, too which I am forever grateful.

It was through this descendant's contact at the British Museum that I was granted access to the archives room and the spectacular *Flora Delanica*. I had my opportunity. Three years and several oceans crossed since my first encounter with Delany and I was back in London for *Wreath*, a solo exhibition at my UK gallery, New Art Projects. By this point I'd already made several monumental drawings and was working on a series of new ceramics in reference to her. It struck me then how only two pieces could fuel such a passion; it was a Rose and a Thistle, or was it a Narcissus?

Re-encounter
I was permitted by strict museum rules to look through one folder, somewhere around 35 works. I appreciated the protocols of handling, feeling queasy breathing the same air—they are after all 250 years old and made of highly delicate materials. Upon very close inspection, I was able to see Delany's lyrical, methodical and truly exquisite hand and eye at work. The images seem to almost undulate at times. The slight gradations of colour; perhaps seven differentiated shades of green slits of paper in a single sprite of dangly leaves, all producing the effect of dimensionality and movement, and almost always against that seductive black background. The intangible depth of her shifts in colour in these specimens are perfectly enveloped by the rich baroque blackness she sets them against, the endless black *pool* of an indeterminate night. My forearm hair is on end thinking about the experience as I recall it in words.

I've been struck before with Stendhal Syndrome, Delany was different. On previous occasions I'd been aware of the art and of the status of the creator, because they'd been engendered for kings and popes, and the majority of them were men. This extraordinary body of work (nearly 1000 individual paper-cuts comprise *Flora Delanica*) were clearly made by Delany a woman, *for Delany*. These are epic love poems to the flowers themselves, minutely tuned to honouring the genius of forms found in the natural world. Each specimen is a sitter, articulated in paper, pigment, scissors and even organic plant materials (bits of the subjects themselves?) with the affectionate eye of a most gifted observer. Often referred to as 'paper-cuts', these might be retrospectively, considered *collage*, based on her ingenious addition of actual plant-materials.

Mary Delany began these works at the age of 72. Think of her vision, dexterity, her clarity of perception, and her playfulness. Her eyes and her hands were mature to the world—but with an extraordinary fitness. In a time when so much is geared toward youth culture, Delany's work is refreshing. These are small works, but they fill one's mind; they affect the entire body. I suppose that is why my own response to Delany in drawing has been on such a large scale. The Pool Series in part, articulates this immensity, where flora, both generated from life and memory mingle in a sort of coital. Some unearthed with exposed roots, others cleanly cut like a deliberately sculpted Delany slice, hovering in blackness, or do they float- or are they sinking? I think they can be seen to do all of the above, and they are all stand-ins for the Human body; the self, that inseparable aspect of the landscape; body is land; land is personal.

Acknowledgements

Essay, "Paper, Petals, Leaves and Skin: A Chance Encounter With the Affectionate Eye of Mary Delany" published in *Antennae, The Journal of Nature in Visual Culture*, Issue 51, Summer 2020

The following poems were previously published in the Chapbook *Euology for the Bouyant*, JackPine Press, 2010.

"Virgo Moon"
"The Grave of Oscar Wilde"
"The Other Side"
"Faerie Tale"
"Sleepy City"
"Posture"
"The Cloud Spitter"
"Horror Poems: Orphanage"
"Things to Remember When I Die"

Thank-yous

A special thank-you to Adrienne Gruber for her dedication, genius, friendship and her honesty during the editing process.

A second special thank-you to several teachers, one of whom is my Mother; who was instrumental in helping me to learn to read and write as a dyslexic.

Zachari Logan is a queer Canadian settler poet and artist whose art has been exhibited in group and solo exhibitions throughout North America, Europe and Asia. Logan's work can be found in collections worldwide, including the National Gallery of Canada, Art Gallery of Ontario, Remai Modern and the Nerman MOCA among many others. In 2014 Logan received the Lieutenant Governor's Emerging Artist Award, in 2015 he received the Alumni of Influence Award from the University of Saskatchewan and in 2016 Logan was long-listed for the Sobey Award. In 2010, his chapbook, *A Eulogy for the Buoyant*, was published by JackPine Press. Logan's artwork and writing has been featured in many publications throughout the world. Zachari Logan lives in Regina, Saskatchewan.